The Ghost of my Pussycat's Bottom

The Ghost of my Pussycat's Bottom

Mike Jubb

Copyright © Mike Jubb 2006
ISBN: 1-904529-23-2

The right of Mike Jubb to be identified as the author of this work has been asserted in accordance with Sections 77 and 78 or the Copyright Designs and Patents Act 1988.

All characters in this publication are fictitious and any resemblance to real persons, living or dead, is purely coincidental.

All rights reserved.
No part of this publication may be reproduced, stored in a retrieval system, or transmitted, in any form or by any means, without the prior permission in writing of the publisher, nor be otherwise circulated in any form of binding or cover other than that in which it is published and without a similar condition including this condition being imposed on the subsequent purchaser

A catalogue record for this book is available from the British Library.

Published by Back To Front
www.back-to-front.com

Here are some poems about all sorts of creatures;
Some of them pets, and some of them wild;
There are some that are mythical, some that are silly,
And some that would eat you... you sweet little child!
(Yum Yum Slurp!)

So, I hope you enjoy this mixture of poems,
But remember that poetry starts at home.
And, if you don't think that they're worth the money,
You can all clear off... and write you own!
(And I hope you will.)

For Tony Bradman
Many thanks for being the first
to give help and encouragement

Contents

1   Author's note

3   **Mostly Cats**
      4   Cats
      5   My Cat is Dead
      6   Cool Cat
      8   Who Gave that Cat a Violin, Anyway?
      10   The Ghost of my Pussycat's Bum
      11   Midnight Meeting

13   **Creepy Crawlies**
      14   Minibeasts
      15   The Death's Head Moth
      16   They're Crawling in my Hair
      18   Till Death Us Do Part
      20   Camilla Caterpillar
      21   The Dung Beetle
      22   Said an Angry Amoeba called Anne
      23   A Worm's Lament
      24   Tina

27   **A Bunch of Birds**
      28   A Quiet Young Duck from Quebec
      29   The Emperor and the Nightingale
      30   Chanticleer and Reynard
      32   The Spirit of the Lark
      33   Unrattled
      34   Polar Bears and Penguins
      35   Love a Dove

37 Some Frogs and a Toad
    38   Froggie Went a'Courting
    39   Some Day my Prince
    40   Limerick and Variations
    41   It's Raining Bats and Frogs
    42   Slow Toad, Fast Car
    43   Taking Time Out

45 Animal Allsorts
    46   The Green Unicorn
    48   Wherever the Blue Whale Goes
    48   A Tiger who Lived in the Zoo
    48   Do Animals Understand?
    49   Badgers
    50   Miss Fossil's Terror Dactyl
    52   Shark Attack
    54   The Tale of the Farmer's Wife
    56   Ho Ho Ho
    57   The Cliché Monster
    58   Jimmy
    60   Adagio e Presto
    61   Bareback Riding

63 Neither Man nor Beast
    64   Flesh Creeper
    65   The Goat-god Pan
    66   The Huntress
    68   The Centaur
    70   The Medusa

71   Here be Dragons
   72   What is a Dragon Like?
   73   George Knight and the Dragon
   74   I Hate to See a Grown Dragon Cry
   75   The Dragon Lord
   76   Sir Bart and the Dragon
   78   The Dragon's Barbeque Rap
   80   An Old Dragon Dreams
   81   Mirror, Mirror
   83   Was it a Cat I Saw

Hi, I'm Mike Jubb.

Welcome to my book of poems about all sorts of creatures. Many of them are meant to be funny, but I've also snuck in a few (oh no!) serious ones because... well, because I wanted to, so there!

When I was young, I was useless at writing. I could never think what to write. No confidence. In fact, I didn't try to write regularly until I was an old man... nearly 40! Now, I spend a lot of time going into schools to perform my poems, and to help children write creatively. I hope that means I'm worth listening to, because I know what it's like to stare at an empty page and think, *I can't do it.*

The truth is... you **can** do it. First, stop worrying about getting it 'wrong.' You can't get it wrong. It's not Maths! Next, be brave enough to write down the first things that come into your head. Don't worry about whether they're any good or not. It's better to write rubbish than to write nothing at all. I often write rubbish! Remember that the best chocolate starts with a load of old beans!

Once you've written something, and you don't have to stare at an empty page any more, you can try to improve it. Like playing football, or netball, or a musical instrument, the more you practise the better you'll get. Soon, you'll be writing **good** rubbish, like me!

People often ask where writers get their ideas from. Everywhere. It helps if I concentrate on keeping my eyes and ears open, and my mouth shut! I learn more that way. And I don't eat as much junk television as I used to! I gobble up programmes about the real world: wildlife, history, travel. Underneath some of my poems, I talk about where the idea came from, and sometimes I suggest some writing that you might like to try.

If you want to write poetry (I mean **really** want to), you have to work at it. First, you need a place where you won't be disturbed. I like to sit in a cafe where nobody knows me, but mostly I just shut myself in my office, or I go to the library. Next, you need the tools of the trade: pen, notebook, a good thesaurus and the Penguin Rhyming Dictionary. The Rhyming Dictionary is essential, for me. I just look up a word, like 'cat', and it tells me all the words that rhyme. It saves so much time.

Writing good rhyming poetry is much harder than writing non-rhyming poetry. You have to think about the rhyme, the rhythm and the meaning. It's easy to shove in any old rhyme, but always remember that the meaning is the most important thing. So, you often have to work at finding the right combination. For example, if I want to find a rhyme for *shout* and there isn't one that fits the meaning I want, then I might have to change *shout* to *yell* or *holler*. Then I've got a whole new set of rhyming words to choose from. Writing is often about solving problems.

I hope you find something in this collection that will encourage you, something that will inspire you and, more than anything else, something that will entertain you.

Happy reading, and confident writing.

Mike.

www.mikejubb.co.uk

Mostly Cats

Cats

Cats are soft and furry, but
    they leave hairs on the sofa.
Cats are playful, but
    they dig their claws into you.
Cats are elegant, but
    they kill birds.

Cats are confusing.

This is what I call a good/bad poem. You decide what you're going to write about, then you think of some 'good' things, and some 'not so good' things about your subject. Three of each is probably enough. Then, you make a kind of pattern with them, and try to come up with a good ending.

Have a go yourself. You can write about almost anything, or anybody!

Here's a couple of ideas to get you started:

> My Mum is... but she...
> Snow is great for... but...

My Cat is Dead

My cat is dead. I have no cat,
though the catflap is still in the door.
It's very important you understand this:
I don't have a cat any more.

She died just over a year ago;
it was simply old age, said the vet.
But I'm terrified now to admit what I fear:
I'm being haunted by my old pet.

It started about a week ago;
goose pimples covered my skin
when the catflap opened, and then swung shut,
but nothing was seen to come in.

Outside, it was raining and blowing a gale;
did the howling wind rattle the door?
My question was answered before I could speak,
as pawprints appeared on the floor.

I seemed to be stuck, with my mouth open wide;
the memory still torments me.
before I could move, or think what to do,
some hidden thing rubbed up against me.

Every last part of me wanted to run,
but my feet were fixed to the floor.
I'm not a brave man, and I shook with fear
when I felt the scratch of a claw.

I'm starting to get used to it now:
the meows inside my...
excuse me, but I have to go;
she's calling me to be fed.

Cool Cat

Well I'm a cat with nine
And I'm in my prime
I'm Casanova Cat
And I'm feline fine
I'm strollin' down the street
In my white slipper feet
Yeh, all the little lady cats
Are lookin' for a treat
Because I got style
I got a naughty smile
I'm gonna cross this street
In just a little while
    to be with you
    to be with you
    to be with you
    to be with
You got grace
You got a lickable face
I'm gonna love ya and leave ya
And you'll never find a trace
Because I'm on my own
I like to be alone
I'm just a swingin', strollin',
Rollin' stone

But it's your lucky day
I'm gonna pass your way
I can spare a little lovin'
If you wanna stop and
    play with me
    play with me
    play with me
    play with
Meeeeow my
I got a twinklin' eye
I'm gonna cross this street
So don't you be too shy
But what's this I see
Comin' straight at me
It's a crazy car driver
Tryin' to make me flee
So I look up slow
Just to let the man know
That I don't go any faster
Than I really wanna…

X!X!X!X!X!X!X!X!X!X!

Well I'm a cat with eight
I guess he couldn't wait
But I'm lookin' good
And I'm feline great!

Who Gave that Cat a Violin, Anyway?

The crazy cat scraped on her fiddle,
The little dog covered his ears;
'That maniac mog gets no better,
though she's practised it for years.'

The stupid cow stood on the hilltop,
And waited for the moon to rise;
She launched herself with all her might,
And sailed into the sky.

When no-one else was looking,
The dish ran away with the spoon;
And you wouldn't believe the things they did
In Bognor, on their honeymoon.

The stupid cow jumped right over the moon,
Nothing unusual in that;
But she landed rather awkwardly,
And squashed the crazy cat.

The little dog laughed to see such fun,
Cos laughter is good for your health;
The trouble is, he laughed so much
He wet his silly self.

But when the fun was over,
A tear or two was shed;
They cremated the cat in the morning,
Just to make sure she was dead.

'There's only us two,' said the stupid cow,
'We must be brave and strong.'
'I'll miss that cat,' sighed the little dog,
'But not for very long.'

They had a postcard from Bognor,
From the two who ran away;
It seems they were having a wonderful time
With the rest of the cutlery tray.

Now, the trouble with writing a story
Is knowing where it should end;
Well, the cow and the dog lived a quiet life
Without their other friends.

But sometimes at night, when the moon is high.
They sit and sing Hey Diddle Diddle;
Then the ghost of that crazy cat comes around,
And scrapes on its flaming fiddle.

I got the idea for this from a wonderful poem called 'The Man in the Moon stayed up too late' by J.R.R.Tolkien. That's right, he wrote Lord of the Rings. He wrote some great poems too, in a collection called 'The Adventures of Tom Bombadil'. It's brilliant.

There's another poem in this book that was inspired by a nursery rhyme. Why don't you have a go yourself? What was Humpty Dumpty doing up on top of the wall in the first place? The twit! And as for the silly girl who lost a whole flock of sheep! Perhaps they were playing Peep Bo with her!

The Ghost of my Pussycat's Bum

When my moggy got sliced through the middle,
She ran out of lives, all nine;
It was bloody and yucky and gruesome,
So I'll tell you about it... next time.

Her front end went straight to cat heaven,
Where ferocious dogs are banned;
But her rear end had often been naughty,
So her bum has to wander the land.

When my cat was alive, in the mornings
She would snuggle beside me in bed,
And she'd nuzzle her nose in my ear-hole;
Now her bum comes to visit instead.

I tell you, it's quite disconcerting
When I'm lying around at my place,
And half of a ghost cat comes creeping
And shoves its bum in my face.

And then, when I open the curtains,
And think what the new day will bring,
The bum lifts its tail towards heaven,
And it does an unspeakable thing!

It's something I'll never get used to,
Cos my moggy was always good fun;
Now it seems that I'm doomed to be haunted
By the ghost of my pussycat's bum.

Midnight Meeting

On soft, silent, padded paws,
all cats are grey in the night;
this is their time.

A shadow walking in shadows,
Prometheus is on the prowl.
Other toms keep their distance,
and a fox crosses the road
to avoid him;
but the mouse saw nothing,
heard nothing,
knew nothing.

On wings without a whisper,
old Tawny perches
on the chimney pot
in time to see the cat
snatch his prey.
Their eyes meet,
the owl and the pussycat,
the staring match of all time.

Prometheus looks away first.
After all,
he has the mouse.

The Owl and the Pussycat by Edward Lear is one of my favourite poems. Real owls and cats are very good at staring without blinking, so one day I had this idea of setting up a poetic staring match between the two. See if you can find out who the real Prometheus was.

Creepy Crawlies

Minibeasts

Creatures of the summer term:
Sliding slugs and wiggling worms;
Spiders spinning silky nets,
Crickets playing castanets;
Woodlice in their armour squeeze
Under stones and fallen trees,
While millipedes and centipedes
Scurry round at such a speed;
Up the bank and down the ditch;
But, tell me, which leg follows which?
And as they're busy counting feet,
The caterpillar has to eat
And eat, and eat, because she must
Get fat until she's fit to bust.

There's ants and ladybirds, and snails
That leave their silvery trails.

There's butterflies we all admire,
And dragonflies that **don't** breathe fire.

Yellow and black can signal 'Danger'
So treat the wasp just like a stranger.

There's beetles, bugs and busy bees,
And many, many more than these.
They run and fly and hop and squirm;
These creatures of the summer term.

If you want to write rhyming poetry, remember that you can 'run on' from one line to the next without stopping. For example, 'Woodlice in their armour squeeze under stones and fallen trees.' This is called *enjambment*, and it helps poets to avoid a rumpty tumpty rhythm (if they want to).

The Death's Head Moth

Keep away from the Black Widow spider,
It has a poisonous bite;
Keep away from the snake that rattles;
But the Death's Head Moth is all right.

Keep away from the stinging jellyfish,
It isn't a good swimming mate;
Keep away from the bad-tempered scorpion;
But the Death's Head Moth is great.

The Death's Head Moth is harmless,
But it certainly isn't dull;
In case you've never seen one,
It looks like a flying skull.

You know what I'm going to say now, don't you? That's right… see if you can find a picture of a Death's Head Moth. I think it should be called the Pirate Moth… now there's an idea for a poem or story!

They're Crawling in my Hair

They're crawling in my hair;
They're driving me out of my wits;
Giving me no peace,
These headlice and these nits.

They've been racing all around,
Like a snowman on a motorbike;
My hair is very clean,
But that's just what they like.

I've been scratching through the night;
They're giving me the itchy-coo;
And now I've got to use
This stinky old shampoo.

I rub with all my might;
I'm hoping this will do the trick;
But the smell of this shampoo
Is making me feel sick.

Later on, when it's dry,
Mummy combs my hair;
Lots and lots of eggs and bodies
Everywhere.

They were crawling in my hair;
They were driving me out of my wits;
Giving me no peace,
Those headlice and those nits.

This idea came from my son, Kevin. When he was little, I took him, and my daughter Nicky, to hear a performance of story music. The story was about a boy who built a snowman which came alive! On the way back, Kevin sang me the first line of this song. You may think that you know the tune, but I couldn't possibly comment.

Till Death Us Do Part

A praying mantis spent his life
searching for the perfect wife,
dreaming of a lovely bride
who'd always pray right by his side.
He wanted nothing more than this:
a happy home, a special kiss,
and, oh, the opportunity
to have a little family...
even if it cost him quids
to be the dad of sixty kids.

Well, he wandered round from tree to tree
to find the female who would be
the loving wife and mother who
would help to make his dreams come true.
But, sometimes, he just sadly sat
and yearned for Love so badly that
he knew that he'd give all he had
to be a husband and a dad.
'For just the chance to have a wife
I'd gladly risk my lonely life.'

And then one happy day he found,
praying high above the ground,
Margery, a mantis miss
who offered him a **special** kiss
and cuddle that would make him smile,
(if only for a little while!).
So bold she was, his face turned red;
'We must get married first,' he said.
'I like to do things proper, so...'
'I will,' she said. 'Come on, let's go!'

With Love our hero was so stricken;
but the 'cuddle' though was such a quick'n!
In his impatience to be mated,
I fear that he miscalculated,
and hardly had the marriage started
than Margery said, 'We must be parted.'
He said, 'I want to share with you my life.'
'And so you shall dear,' smiled his wife.
She kissed him sweetly on the nose,
then started biting off his toes.

'Before I start to lay the eggs,'
she said, 'I fancy scrambled legs.'
This made our hero quite distraught:
'So this is married life,' he thought.
It wasn't easy to forgive her
while she was lunching on his liver,
and saying that it was her intention
to eat the bits I dare not mention.
And as she crunched his tearful head,
'You've been a good husband to me,' she said.

It's a tragedy!

You want to know where ideas come from? Watch wildlife programmes on telly. They are full of good starting places for writing. Especially if you've got a wicked mind like mine!

Camilla Caterpillar

Camilla Caterpillar kept a caterpillar killer-cat;
A caterpillar killer categorically she kept.
But alas the caterpillar killer-cat attacked Camilla
As Camilla Caterpillar catastrophically slept.

This is a fairly tricky tongue twister (try to say it fast!). But, from a writer's point of view, there's lots going on in this poem. There's all the alliteration: cat, caterpillar, kept, Camilla, killer, categorically, catastrophically. Four of those words even start with 'cat'.

There's rhyme with 'kept' and 'slept'; there's *internal* rhyme with 'caterp*illar*', 'Cam*illa*' and 'k*iller*'; and then there's 'catastrophically' and 'categorically', both six syllable words that sort of echo as well as rhyme.

Many of the words have the 'a' sound inside them. When this happens, it's called 'assonance'. And lastly, the word 'attacked' also has several sounds that echo in other words. It even has the word 'cat' backwards!

Why am I going on about it? Because this short poem took many hours to write… from the moment I started to collect words together, through many drafts, searching for better words, until I came to the point where I don't think I could possibly improve on it. I'm not saying it's the perfect poem, but it's probably the nearest I'll ever get.

The Dung Beetle

What fun to be a dung beetle
rolling balls of dung;
so soft and slightly pungent
in the heat of the midday sun.

When other creatures hide away,
or in the shade go flopping,
I race around excitedly
and try to find a dropping.

Elephant poop is best, of course,
it makes the finest spheres;
especially when it's steaming hot,
I dive in up to my ears.

I dig some out, and roll it up,
I'm careful not to waste it.
Sometimes a bit gets in my mouth,
you really ought to taste it.

Uphill, it's a struggle to push it home,
but downhill is OK;
I just grab hold and cling on tight,
And wheeeeee! I'm on my way.

Oh, such fun to be a dung beetle
rolling balls of dung;
so soft and slightly pungent
in the heat of the midday sun.

Said an Angry Amoeba called Anne

Said an angry amoeba called Anne,
'I'm going as fast as I can;
But with only one cell,
It's annoying as hell
That I'll never reach Spain or Japan.'

I expect you know that this form of poetry is called a limerick. Writing limericks is great fun. It's also a good way of getting into rhyming poetry because it has a clear structure to build on, a bit like the frame that holds a tent up. All you have to do is come up with an idea, then work at finding the right words to fit the frame. You could organise a limerick competition at school. Get the whole school writing them... including your teachers!

A Worm's Lament

With a Mistle Thrush on one end
And a Mistle Thrush on t'other,
It were just my luck to get **two** early birds.
What with that one pullin' this way
And this one pullin' that,
A worm could use some **very** naughty words.

I suppose you think it's funny
That I'm in a tug of war;
Caught between two beaks that think I'm caviar.
And neither one is giving way,
They've both set out to win;
But I just think it's stretching things **too** far!

Unfortunately, we don't see as many Mistle Thrushes as we used to. They like to hunt for food in short grass. If a worm is daft enough to be poking out of its hole, the thrush nabs it and starts pulling with all its might, while the worm tries to hang on for dear life! It can get a bit stretched! So, you can imagine what it would be like with a thrush on *both* ends!

Tina

It's the only time I've ever heard Dad scream.

Of course,
we all **knew** that he hated spiders, and
he never wanted me to have one in the **first** place,

but Mum said
she had a pet spider,
(when she was young)
and she couldn't see any reason
why **I** shouldn't have one too.

And, anyway, Tina isn't a very **big** Tarantula.

I can't imagine **how** she could have escaped.
Or how she managed to get all the way
to Dad's bedroom.

And, anyway, Dad shouldn't still have been in bed
at that time of day.

Of course,
it was worse because **he** thought
that it was **Mum**
who was tickling his nose.

Dad doesn't shout much usually.
But boy, can he SCREAM!

Did you notice that I don't actually *tell* you what happened. It's all hints and suggestions. Sometimes that can be the best way to build a picture in your reader's mind.

There are hundreds of poems waiting to be written about pets, from simple descriptions of them… to the funny things they do… to fantasy stories about them… to nightmares about them! Just suppose you woke up one morning and *you* were *their* pet!

A Bunch of Birds
(with polar bears, a fox and...
who let that cat in here?)

A Quiet Young Duck from Quebec

A quiet young duck from Quebec
Can't quack cos his nerves are a wreck;
He may quiver and quake,
But no sound can he make.
Or perhaps it's the knot in his neck.

I wrote this limerick for a book that wasn't published in the end. The idea was that I had to find a way of emphasising the sound 'qu'.

I enjoy having restrictions like that sometimes. It helps me to concentrate, and to work at finding the best words for the job.

Try giving yourself a subject, such as *Mice* or *Snow* or *Anger*, and see how many different poems you can write about it. Four of the Dragon poems, at the end of this book, were all written on the same day.

The Emperor and the Nightingale

Silent nightingale:
the cage that you occupy
is not the whole world.

Sad, lonely songbird
treated like a clockwork toy:
sing inside your head.

No consolation:
the Emperor too is trapped,
with no song to sing.

Did you notice that each stanza of this poem is a haiku? When haiku are linked in this way, it's called a *rensaku*.

This poem was partly inspired by the fairytale 'The Emperor and the Nightingale', and partly by a line in the poem 'November' by John Clare. He's talking about a really foggy day when a ploughman couldn't even see his horse in front of the plough:

> *So dull and dark are the November days.*
> *The lazy mist high up the evening curled,*
> *And now the morn quite hides in smoke and haze;*
> *The place we occupy seems all the world.*

Chanticleer and Reynard

Chanticleer was a cockerel,
Big-headed and so proud;
He couldn't sing for toffee,
But, Boy! His mouth was loud!

Old Reynard was a crafty fox,
He could charm, and he could flatter;
He wanted Chanticleer for lunch,
Dipped in a spicy batter.

Now Chanticleer was roosting
On his perch up in a tree;
He couldn't fly, so he must have climbed;
Now **that** would be something to see!

The crafty fox came creeping by
As the cockerel crowed the day;
'What a beautiful song,' said Reynard,
'But far too quiet, I'd say.'

'If you would just come down and sing
 For me, it would be grand;
And if you sing your loudest,
I'll let you join my band.'

So Chanticleer, all puffed with pride,
He fluttered down, but what a shock;
The old fox pounced and gobbled him up,
The stupid little cock.

So, if you're proud or boastful,
I hope you see the light;
Chanticleer was fooled by flattery,
And it served him stuffing-well right.

The story of Chanticleer and the fox goes back hundreds of years. There are various versions, but probably the best is called *The Nun's Priest's Tale,* from *The Canterbury Tales* by Geoffrey Chaucer. In that one, the cockerel escapes… but not here!

The spirit of the lark

My wing is broken, cried the Lark,
I cannot rise to sing;
I cannot soar above the Downs
By Chanctonbury Ring.

I cannot mend your broken wing,
The sighing wind replied.
The Lark, it seemed, gave up all hope,
And, broken-hearted, died.

Yet, on the wind, above the Downs,
By Chanctonbury Ring.
The soaring spirit of the Lark
May still be heard to sing.

Chanctonbury Ring is the remains of an iron age hill fort, about 240 metres high, on the South Downs in West Sussex. When you're up there on a sunny Spring day, and you hear a skylark singing, it's just magical.

Don't ask me where this poem came from. It just arrived, and told me to write it down. So I did. I think it's about not letting The Meanies of life beat you; and also keeping your sense of freedom alive, even when you're locked up... like dreaming of being in the park when you have to stay in and do your homework!

Unrattled

Two rattling magpies
machine-gun their anger
from a branch
in the horse chestnut.

Passing under the tree,
the cause of this clackety-racket
pauses, yawns,
twitches a contemptuous tail
then pads silently on,
pretending not to notice.

Have you ever stopped to listen to magpies when they've got a lot to say for themselves, especially when something is upsetting them? They don't sound *exactly* like machine guns, but that's what they remind me of.

Of course, I haven't actually said what's making them cross here... but I think you've got a pretty good idea. Cats sometimes make it very difficult for you to ignore them, but they're expert at taking no notice of you.

Polar Bears and Penguins

Polar bears and penguins
Playing the snow;
You see it on your Christmas cards,
But don't the artists know
That polar bears live northwards
In the Arctic all the year,
And penguins only hang out
In the southern hemisphere?

So listen all you artists,
You're making me uptight;
THEY NEVER MEET EACH OTHER!
So get it flippin' right!

I don't think that this poem needs any explanation, but it's another example of an idea just waiting around to be noticed. Most writers always have a notebook with them so that when an idea goes 'tingaling!' in their head, they can jot it down for using later.

Love a Dove

Three baby doves
were saved from
starvation...

after bird lover,
Mary Frink,
63, of Suffolk,
let them eat food

out of her mouth.

This is a 'found' poem. I found this interesting snippet in a newspaper. It just took my fancy so, without changing any words, I set them out to look like a piece of free verse, and I gave it a title. See what *you* can find. As well as newspapers and magazines, you could try looking in non-fiction books. I once 'wrote' one on how to make a mummy. Not nice!

Some Frogs and a Toad

Froggie Went a'Courting

Up to the house of young Miss Mouse
A frog went courting one day;
But why would he fancy a rodent?
He must have been kinky that way.

When the frog and the mouse got married,
She loved him, and he loved her;
But can you imagine their children?
All covered in green slimy fur.

The story of a frog courting a mouse is a traditional one. When I use an old tale for inspiration, I try to find a different 'angle' to write from.

This poem is begging for more verses to be written. Go on, have a go!

Some Day, My Prince

      Kiss . . . . . Croak
      Kiss . . . . . Croak
      Kiss . . . . . Croak
      Kiss . . . . . Croak

I'll find that flipping Prince
if I have to kiss
every frog in this pond.

Limerick and Variations

A foolish young Princess relied
On having a Prince by her side.
So she started to snog
With a slimy old frog,
But the poor creature withered and died.

■   ■   ■

A Princess, who couldn't kiss frogs,
Tried hamsters and horses and dogs.
Then she hugged and she kissed
With a creature that hissed,
But it squeezed till she popped off her clogs.

■   ■   ■

A dark-haired young Princess was fond
Of kissing a frog in the pond.
But it made the frog wince
Cos he wasn't a prince,
And besides that, he wanted a blonde.

You can seen I had fun with this idea. But, I'm sure there are many more ways of writing about a Princess who kisses a frog. Now that *is* kinky!

It's Raining Bats and Frogs

It's raining bats and frogs.
Above the clouds,
all the witches and wizards of the world are
hurling spells of change at each other,
like snowballs.

Dead crows
fall from the sky.
Snakes of lightning
with forked tongues
fang the earth.
Bats clatter into walls, frogs try to fly,
and exploding toads splatter
onto the roads below.

Slowly,
slowly,
like black snowflakes,
a million million spiders
come parachuting
silently
into your life.

I'm sure you don't need me to tell you that the first idea for this poem came from the traditional saying, 'It's raining cats and dogs'. After changing that to bats and frogs, I asked myself the question Why?

Answer: a battle of magic is going on in the sky. It's important to ask yourselves questions as a writer… because it forces you to give an answer. When you've got an answer, you've got something to write.

The Slow Toad and the Fast Car

Old toad,
cold and warty,
creeps across the road,
couldn't give a toss
about left and right.

Fast car,
hot-headed
and sporty-red;
speeding eyes in the night.

Old toad
makes it to the middle.
Fast car
shakes the air;
doesn't care.

Old toad,
really a witch.
Fast car,
in the ditch.

One of the things that makes poetry different from prose is that, in poetry, you don't have to write in proper sentences. You can also leave out words if they're not really important. So, for example, in the last part of this poem there are two 'sentences', but no verbs.

In a story, I would have to write something like: *The old toad was really a witch, and she magically made the fast car crash into a ditch.* Too many words for poetry; eighteen instead of ten. My rule of thumb is: if you can get rid of any words, and the poem doesn't miss them, then chuck 'em out. Same for prose too.

Taking Time Out

Taking time out from chaos;
from trying to hold it all together,
>   while others put on him
>   demand from him
>   misunderstand him
>   abuse him
>   confuse him
>   bash him and
>   send him crashing.

And that's only his friends.

Taking time out from
>   being the one that
>   they all turn to;
>   the one that
>   they all take for granted.

Taking time for himself:
>   trying to make sense
>   of all the nonsense.
Sitting alone, legs dangling,
Losing, then finding, himself in a song;
A song from his heart to yours:

It's not easy being green.

I'm taking a risk here that you've seen Kermit the frog sitting and singing by his beloved swamp. He sings 'It's not easy being green,' and it almost sounds as though he doesn't like himself very much. I sometimes feel like singing, 'It's not easy being me.' But it's important to like yourself and, by the end of the song, Kermit realises that he should be proud of who he is: someone who does his best when doing your best isn't... well... easy.

Animal Allsorts

The Green Unicorn

He came with the storm.

On Monday,
he evaporated all weapons
as though they had never been invented.

On Tuesday,
he turned all cars and lorries
into bicycles and milk floats.

On Wednesday,
he destroyed all polluting factories
and he refreshed the air.

On Thursday,
he cleansed the lakes and the seas
and he breathed life into dead rivers.

On Friday,
he freed all zoo animals
and returned them to renewed homelands.

On Saturday,
he took a little from those that had much
and gave much to those that had little.

On Sunday,
he tried to share his love with every heart,
but he was weary
and couldn't be sure that he had reached them all.

He left with the wind,
and he whispered to the World,
'Now have another try.'

Milk floats were slow, electric vehicles, used to deliver milk to our homes. My thought in this stanza was to find ways of slowing life down a bit.

This is a wishful thinking sort of poem. Unfortunately, no green unicorn is going to clean up the world for us. We must do it ourselves.

Limericks are usually written to be funny, but I've been experimenting with using the limerick pattern for other feelings. See what you think.

Wherever the Blue Whale Goes

Wherever the Blue Whale goes,
Whatever the water he blows,
He whistles his song
As he swims along,
Or whispers the tale of his woes.

■ ■ ■

A Tiger who Lived in the Zoo

A tiger who lived in the zoo
Died of boredom and feeling blue;
But his happy ghost roams
Through the jungle alone,
Which was all that he wanted to do.

■ ■ ■

Do Animals Understand?

Do animals understand
The damage we do to their land?
Does the ostrich see
That it's really we
Who are hiding our heads in the sand.

Badgers

**Brock meets brock in a Wiltshire wood
After dark, to forage for food;
Digging around for a bite to eat:
Grubs and other tasty treats.
Earthworms are their choice delight.
Rummaging raiders; with black and white
Stripes in the night. Stripes in the night.**

In case you've never heard the word, 'brock' is a country name for a badger. Near my home, in Hampshire, there's a Brockhurst, and a Brockenhurst ('hurst' means 'wood').

I expect you've written acrostics at school. This one started off simply, but then I decided to work a bit harder and turn it into a rhyming one. Did you notice that 'wood' and 'food' don't exactly rhyme? It doesn't matter. Near-rhymes can work just as well, or even better.

49

Miss Fossil's Terror Dactyl

The word 'despicable' would be applicable
to Miss Fossil's Terror Dactyl.

With a bat's skill
with an acrobat's thrilling nimble-tumble through the air,
with a feral cat's shrill screech,
Miss Fossil's Terror Dactyl spills off the windowsill and
fills each pupil (her dear little children!) with
a brat-chilling fear.

They will behave.

And there will be no grumbling, because
Miss Fossil's Terror Dactyl has a bumble-bee needle-sting.
And its belly rumbles.

And there will be no crying, because
like a demented flying turtle,
Miss Fossil's Terror Dactyl hurtles past your ear,
a mad thing
bombilating uncontrollably;
and a child's sad eyes dare not drop even one tear
for fear of a surprise reprisal from
Miss Fossil's abominable Terror Dactyl.

And there will be no backchat, because
its bill can drill a hole through... well,
let's not think about that.
Or the smell.

Its habitat is the classroom.
It can quell and coerce
the most rebellious little...
person.
At the first sniff of a squabble,
the first whiff of aggravation,
Miss Fossil burbles a verbal signal to her Terror Dactyl,
and the situation for that person
will worsen.

Miss Fossil's Terror Dactyl is terrible,
unbearable.
Miss Fossil's Terror Dactyl is formidable,
unforgiving
and unforgivable.
Miss Fossil's Terror Dactyl is older than rocks,
colder than ice.
Miss Fossil's Terror Dactyl is bolder than crocodiles;
it never smiles
and it's not nice.

Miss Fossil's Terror Dactyl is
on your shoulder.

No prizes for guessing that the idea for my invented Terror Dactyl came from playing with the word *pterodactyl*. I like experimenting with words, and in this poem I've experimented a lot with internal rhymes; that is, rhymes that don't fall at the ends of lines. How many can you find?

Shark Attack

The shadowy shape of a *shark*
Will make a *dogfish* bark,
Or make a *catfish* climb a tree in fright.
How the *hake* and *haddock* hustle,
While the *cockle* shows his *mussel*,
And the *dace* must find a *plaice* that's out of sight.

When the shark is on the gobble,
How the *jelly-fish* will wobble,
How the *cuttle-fish* will scuttle to its hole.
But the *crayfish* and the *cod*
Do the *conger*, which is odd;
And the *ray* can only pray to save its *sole*.

When the shark is being sharkish,
All the *shellfish* and the *starfish*
Hide the *winkle* in a twinkle from his jaws.
But the *whiting* will not wait
As the *scallops* try to *skate*,
And the *sea-horse* gallops off to hide indoors.

To avoid old sharky's gullet,
The *mackerel* and the *mullet*
Leave the *roach* and *loach* to *flounder* in the lurch.
But the *tuna* and the *tuny*
Can't see anyfin that's funny
When the *flying fish* falls laughing off its *perch*.

When the shark has had his fill,
And he's feeling rather *brill*,
How the *herring* and the *halibut* will sigh.
How the *turbot* and the *trout*
And the *shad* will give a shout;
But the *crab* will *dab* a teardrop from its eye.

Now the shark has finished fishing,
And the *wrasse* and *bass* are missing,
With the *salmon* and the *sardine* and the *scat*;
Let us find a fishy thought
For those *clownfish* that were caught:
I hope **you** won't be such a silly *spratt*!

This poem came from the single idea: dogfish should bark. After that, it was researching for fish names that could have another meaning, like 'skate' (I love puns). That was the easy bit. Then came hours of hard work trying to craft a fun poem, seeing how many different fish I could squeeze in. I call it 'hard work', but it's more like the work you put into solving a crossword puzzle. I enjoy it, and it's a great feeling when you achieve success.

The Tale of the Farmer's Wife

The clock struck twelve in the farmhouse;
A yellow moon hung overhead.
The old farmer's wife and the farmer
Were upstairs in their four-poster bed.

The farmer was sleeping soundly,
And dreaming of shearing his sheep;
But his wife was tossing and turning;
She couldn't get off to sleep.

All at once, there came a strange wailing;
The farmer's wife sat up in bed.
And there, in the pale yellow moonlight,
Was a sight that filled her with dread.

Three manky mice just walked through the wall,
As the old woman's terror was growing.
They might have come in through the open door,
But they couldn't see where they were going.

The three ghostly mice were struggling
To carry a carving knife;
And each had a tail tucked under its arm,
As they groped for the old farmer's wife.

'We want you, we want you,' they snivelled.
'We want you, we want you tonight.
'We want you,' the three mice repeated,
And the old woman's grey hair turned white.

Closer and closer, the three blind mice
Came waving the carving knife;
The farmer's wife screamed and jumped out of bed,
And started to run for her life.

They all ran after the farmer's wife,
Have you ever seen such a thing?
The little dog laughed to see such fun,
And the birds began to sing.

Out of the farmhouse, into the yard
They followed her through the night;
Over the hills and far away
Till they all disappeared from sight.

When the farmer awoke in the morning,
And found that his wife had gone,
He searched for at least five minutes;
Shrugged his shoulders, and just carried on.

But after the hour of midnight,
When a yellow moon hangs overhead,
The ghosts of his wife and the three blind mice
Come to visit the farmer in bed.

Another poem inspired by a nursery rhyme. I wondered what might happen *after* the rhyme was over. This could be called 'Revenge of the Three Blind Mice!' I'm thinking of writing one called 'Revenge of the Rockabye Baby'. I mean, what idiot would rock a baby in the top of a tree?

Ho Ho Ho
(a tonic for the chronically phonic)

An honest horse
made his home
in a house
on the hot horizon.

Every hour,
he put on a hood,
dipped his hooves in honey,
and hoisted a flag...
to celebrate
eleven different ways of
pronouncing 'ho'.

Silly poem, but I wrote it just to show that the letters 'ho' make many different sounds when they're blended with other letters.

The Cliché Monster

As big as a house,
As quiet as a mouse;
As tough as old boots,
As bald as a coot;
As sly as a fox,
As strong as an ox;
As deaf as a post,
As warm as toast;
As high as a kite,
As dark as night;
As slimy as a snake,
As thin as a rake;
As clear as a bell,

LIKE A BAT OUT OF HELL !

Most times when I write a poem, I collect words and phrases together first. Then, I see what I can do with them. In this case, I was making a list of similes that are also clichés when I noticed that some of them rhymed. The poem was written in a few minutes, and all I had to do then was invent a title that made a kind of sense out of it.

I nearly always add the title last. That way, the title should fit what I've written... instead of trying to write a poem to fit a title.

Jimmy

A dog was what I really wanted.
That's what I used to nag Mum and Dad for.

I bought dog books and dog DVDs
and dog posters and dog key-rings
and dog stickers.
They let me have dog wallpaper
in my bedroom,
and a dog duvet cover.

But they wouldn't let me have a dog.

No matter how much I nagged and pestered,
and wished and dreamed,
no dog.

Then, one day,
my Dad brought home a big cage,
and a rat.

Dad said, 'This is Jimmy. He's for you, if
you stop going on about having a dog.'

Part of me was disappointed, but
most of me fell in love with Jimmy straight away.
He's chocolate and cream and very smart.
He even knows his name and
comes to the door of his cage when I call him.

He's an acrobat, and
I make up tricky trails for him to work out
so he can get a treat.
We play together for hours.

But what I love most about Jimmy is that
he's always pleased to see me, and
he's never cross or mean, and
he never tells me off or shouts at me, and
he never criticizes or tells me not to sulk.

He just loves me all the time.
And I love him, and I look after him.

And I can talk to him about dogs.

Adagio e Presto

A tortoise tends to take his time,
He doesn't have to hurry;
The dandelion can't run away,
So there's no need to worry.

A cheetah, on the other hand,
Is faster on his feet;
He has to speed across the land,
Or else he doesn't eat.

Adagio and *presto* are Italian musical words, meaning 'in slow time' and 'in quick time'. I used them partly to describe the different speeds of the two animals, and partly to show how I think the poem should be performed.

Since I wrote this poem, I've discovered that there's a piece of music called *Adagio e Presto,* by a composer named Pez. It's for alto recorder and piano, but I haven't managed to hear it yet.

Bare Back Riding

I've ridden a New Forest pony,
I've ridden a camel too;
I've ridden a wonky donkey,
And a llama in darkest Peru;
I've ridden a mule in Morocco,
But there's one thing I don't recommend:
That's riding a hedgehog naked,
Cos it don't half hurt your rear end.

The idea for this poem came from a wonderful 1960's radio comedy series called *Round the Horne*. One programme included a sketch in which a small person rode on a hedgehog. Writers steal... I mean borrow... ideas from other writers all the time. The important thing is to make them your own.

Neither Man nor Beast

Flesh Creeper

When the moon is the merest sliver,
And thousands of stars stab the sky,
When Grandfather Toad comes crawling,
So do I.

When there's hardly a sound from the river,
And bats begin to fly,
When the Willow Wolf comes prowling,
So do I.

When even the shadows shiver,
And statues start to cry,
When the Old Owl of Merda comes hunting,
So do I.

So do I.

So, what does the 'Flesh Creeper' look like? The reason I didn't want any illustrations in this book was because I'd like you to use your own imagination. Why should *I* tell you what it looks like... especially when I don't know myself? And anyway, the unknown is much scarier than the things we can see. That's why I always look under my bed at night... just in case!

    The best poem about hidden scary things that I know is *The Mewlips*, by J.R.R. Tolkien.

The Goat-god Pan

When Pan was just a little chap,
He got into an awful flap;
The first time he looked in the lake,
He said, 'There must be some mistake,
I'm neither goat nor hominid,
I'm just a crazy mixed-up kid.' *

The other gods said, rather smugly,
'To us you look extremely ugly;
You must admit it's rather weird
To see a nipper with a beard.
Such hairy legs are somewhat silly;
With horns, you look just like a billy.
We do not mean to be unkind,
But can't you just make up your mind?
Pull yourself together Pan,
Are you goat or are you man?'

Young Pan replied, 'It's cruel to laugh,
I can't help being half and half.
You ought to ask my Dad and Mother
Why I'm not one thing or the other;
Perhaps it comes from being born
Under the sign of Capricorn.
But anyway, you lot can scram
If you can't take me as I am.
When I grow up, it's my ambition
To be the most superb musician.
And as I pipe each peaceful note,
Who'll care if I am man or goat?'

*A kid is young goat. It's a joke. Crazy mixed-up kid... get it?
Oh, suit yourself! Go and see what you can find out about Pan.

The Huntress

The night is cool and dangerous.

The moon rises yellow.

Half in shadow, half in light,
a woman stands under the acacia tree.

The herds of zebra and wildebeest
are quiet.

She steps out.
Keeping upwind,
so they do not smell her,
she crouches down
and crawls.

Creeping low, almost on her belly,
the tall grass
strokes her body.

Nearer. No hurry. Nearer. Patience. Nearer.
So close now,
and they don't even know
she's there.

She's there,
her eyes unblinking,
fixed on the chosen one.

Then,
with a final flick of her tail,
the lioness bounds out of hiding
drags down the wildebeest
and stabs her teeth into its throat.

All I can remember about writing this one is that I pinched the first line from a wildlife programme on telly!

It's back to having an ideas notebook again. Jot down any word or phrase that takes your fancy. Then, on a day when you can't think of anything to write about, go to your notebook, grab an idea and *work* on it.

The Centaur

The Centaur (poor demented soul),
When he was just a boy (or foal),
Of all the many mythical creatures
Had some most unusual features.
Although his form was photogenic,
Alas, he was quite schizophrenic;
Half a horse and half a bloke
Was not his notion of a joke.
This equine/hominoidal fusion
Resulted in his disillusion,
Filling him with such remorse
To think his rear end was a horse.
(I'm sure that it would make **you** glum
to know you had a horse's bum).

'Oh why was I created so?
Whose joke was this, I'd like to know?
Just what am I supposed to be?
It really is confusing me.'

Tormented by these deep divisions,
He found it hard to make decisions;
For not the least of all his cares,
Should he be chasing girls, or mares?
And where to live? He was unable
To choose between a house and stable.
And when he wasn't feeling well,
Who to phone? He couldn't tell.
That was the hardest question yet,
To call the doctor, or the vet?

Neither horse nor humankind,
The Centaur slowly lost his mind;
Until one day the goat-god Pan
Said, 'Don't worry if you're horse or man.
Life can be a lot of fun
When you've got two for the price of one.
Accept yourself for what you are,
And you'll be happier by far.
Take this advice my little friend,
And it will come right in the end.'

The Centaur saw that this was true.
He understood what he must do.
From that day on, his life was changed;
No longer did he feel deranged.
No longer did he whinge and moan,
And he won the Derby on his own.

The Medusa

Medusa's face could turn a man
to stone, for goodness sakes.
She never washed her hair at all,
In case she drowned the snakes.

Myths, legends and folk tales are all good places to look for ideas. Medusa was one of the Gorgons in Greek mythology. She was a beautiful maiden who was cursed by the god Poseidon (because she didn't fancy him!) and he caused her to have live snakes instead of hair. I guess he just couldn't take the rejection!

Another Gorgon invented a new cheese, which she called Ola. Nowadays, we call it Gorgon's Ola! True or false?

Here be Dragons

What is a Dragon Like?

Scaly skin,
Terrible teeth, sharp claws;
With slow flapping wings the dragon comes.

He'll look for you, he'll search for you,
He'll seek you out wherever you hide.
So run fast run.

Can you feel his hot breath
behind you?
Faster run faster.

Flames around your ankles,
red and orange and yellow.
He roars
and the field is on fire.

His sticky tongue licks,
reaches for you, and licks you.

You are going to find out
what a dragon is like

ON THE INSIDE.

Always try to look for a new or different angle when you're writing, so that you can give your reader something that they might not expect. In the next poem, there's a different angle on the story of St George and the Dragon.

George Knight and the Dragon

Chief inspector George Knight
Arrested a dragon for setting light
To the local fire station.
Acting on received information,
George tracked the dragon down
At the Maiden Market, in the old part of town.
The dragon was taken without a struggle;
George surprised him with a fire-proof muzzle,
And locked the beast up in the town jail.
The Magistrate refused to give him bail.
Then the trial was held at the County Court,
The dragon pleaded Guilty, which kept it short.
He said, 'I was trying to blow my snout...
And when I opened my mouth, the flames just shot out.'
George Knight was told, 'You're a hell of a cop!'
And the Judge gave him a strawberry lollipop.
The dragon was told off, and clipped round the ear,
And his fire was put out for two hundred years.
Some people thought that he got off light;
They said that he should have been slain by rights.
Whatever the truth, there's a lesson worth learning;
You can't have flames without something burning.
Maybe the fire *was* an accident... but
It's always best to know when to keep your mouth shut.

I Hate to See a Grown Dragon Cry

I hate to see a grown dragon cry;
Purple teardrops flow from his eyes.
They drip from the end of his sniffing snout,
Cos his girlfriend decided to blow him out,
Yes, I hate to see a grown dragon cry.

It's so sad to see a grown dragon cry;
He sits and he sobs and he sighs.
When she heartlessly told him that they must part,
The fire went out from his brave dragon heart.
So sad to see a grown dragon cry.

There's no comfort when a grown dragon cries;
His hurt seems to whip through the sky.
Then the lightning of pain
Strikes his heart once again,
And that's when a grown dragon dies.

The Dragon Lord

You can't touch me! said the Dragon Lord.
I'm the Mightiest of the Mighty,
with the greatest horde of gold
the world has ever seen.
I'm Invincible, Magnificent,
the most powerful dragon there's ever been.

The Dragon Lord died like a miserable worm;
killed by a microscopic germ.

Notice the rhyme of *horde* with *Lord*. It's not where you'd expect a rhyme to be, is it? The rule with poetry is: **you can make your own rules.**

Sir Bart and the Dragon

In days of old, when knights were bold,
And rode on silver steeds
To rescue maidens in distress,
And other noble deeds,
There was a knight who wouldn't fight
Because he was a rotter;
His name was Sir Bartholemew Augustus Cuthbert Trotter.

Now, this Sir Bart had a poisonous heart.
He thought that it was grand
To see the maidens fleeing
from the dragon in the land.
In his wicked way, he'd smirk and say,
'Oh good, the dragon got her.'
A beast was Sir Bartholemew Augustus Cuthbert Trotter.

One frosty morn, across his lawn
A mother ran to say,
The dragon caught her daughter
And was taking her away.
The mother moaned, 'You've never known
A fairer maid or sweeter.'
But, Bart was cruel, and only drooled,
'Oh let the dragon eat her.'

Now, the dragon heard these wicked words,
And straightway changed his plan.
He knew what maidens tasted like,
So now he'd try a man.
The dragon strode along the road,
To Bart's great house he came;
And he shoved his chops through the letter-box
And breathed a fiery flame.

The dragon's fire made the knight perspire;
The flames were getting hotter
And roasting Sir Bartholemew Augustus Cuthbert Trotter.
How soon Sir Bart was torn apart
As the dragon began to eat.
He was meatier far than the maidens are
But nowhere near as sweet.

The dragon crunched and munched his lunch,
And spat out lumps of gristle.
Till a pain in the gizzard of that loathsome lizard
Made the creature whistle.
He howled and moaned, he growled and groaned
When he realised his mistake;
'twas the poisonous heart of barbarous Bart
That made his belly ache.
He fell on his side, he cried, he died,
And they carted him off in a wagon.
And that was how a miserable coward
Killed that dreadful dragon.

Take a close look at the rhyming scheme in this poem. It wasn't achieved by being satisfied with the first rhymes that came into my head. The poem took many hours of drafting and re-drafting.

The Dragon's Barbecue Rap

I'm a Dragon, Dragon, a big bad Dragon;
Dragon, Dragon, I'm a big bad Dragon;
I'm a big bad, slightly mad, scraggy old fleabag;
Dragon, Dragon, a big bad Dragon;
Dragon, Dragon, I'm a big bad Dragon.

Well how do you do, don't you know my name?
I'm the King of Fire, I'm the King of Flame:
I can cook my meal in a minute or two,
So welcome to... my barbecue.
I don't eat veg, I'm a carnivore,
But I like it cooked, I can't stand it raw;
I can grill your granny, I can roast your dad,
Then I'll cover them with custard... cos I'm slightly mad.

I'm a Dragon, Dragon, a big bad Dragon;
Dragon, Dragon, I'm a big bad Dragon;
I'm a big bad, slightly mad, scraggy old fleabag;
Dragon, Dragon, a big bad Dragon;
Dragon, Dragon, I'm a big bad Dragon.

Eating people is good for my tum;
I can toast your teacher, I can roast your mum,
Then I'll wash them down with a Fiery Fizz,
It's the coolest, hottest drink there is;
That's a tasty snack for a dude like me,
It'll keep me goin' till it's time for tea.
It's a wonderful life, and it makes me glad
When I wake up every morning feeling slightly mad.

Cos I'm a Dragon, Dragon, a big bad Dragon;
Dragon, Dragon, I'm a big bad Dragon;
I'm a big bad, slightly mad, scraggy old fleabag;
Dragon, Dragon, a big bad Dragon;
Dragon, Dragon, I'm a big bad Dragon.

Now here's a lot of kids, but there's gonna be fewer,
When I get four or five of you on my skewer;
Like I said before, I can only eat meat,
And you're the meat that I'm gonna eat.
So how do you feel, now you know my name?
I'm King of the Fire, I'm King of the Flame:
I can cook my meal in a minute or two,
So you're welcome to... my barbecue.

Oh, I'm a Dragon, Dragon, a big bad Dragon;
Dragon, Dragon, I'm a big bad Dragon;
I'm a big bad, slightly mad, scraggy old fleabag;
Dragon, Dragon, a big bad Dragon;

Dragon, Dragon, I'm a big bad DRAGON.

An Old Dragon Dreams

There's a curious story that I have read,
That somewhere in a town called Maidenhead
An old dragon sits in his rocking chair,
And remembers the days when he used to scare
The pants off all the maidens. And some he slew;
Oh yes, in his time, he devoured quite a few.
Knights used to visit, itching for a fight;
But it always finished with... Goodnight Knight!
The fire in his belly was constantly raging;
But over time, as he was ageing,
His wicked old ways didn't seem to matter;
Now he'd much rather sit with a mate, and natter.
Except that his mates are all dead and gone,
And the old dragon knows that it won't be long
Before he goes too.
But there's one last thing that he'd like to do;
If one more time he could summon the power
To capture a maiden that he could devour.
But it's just a dream in an old dragon's head;
The maidens that live in Maidenhead
Are far too quick on their feet to get caught;
And besides, his breath is getting short.
Yet, in his dreams, it's back to the chase;

And the old dragon dies... with a smile on his face.

Mirror, Mirror

Mirror mirror, on the wall
Who's the ugliest dragon of all?

You are, you repulsive reptile!

Oooo, thanks!

Was it a cat I saw
Creeping behind the door?

Can you say this backwards?
wasitacatisaw

Trust a cat to get the last word! Words or phrases that read exactly the same backwards are called palindromes. If you type 'palindromes' into an internet search engine like Google®, you'll find some great ones.

TTFN.

Acknowledgements

I should like to acknowledge that my lovely wife, Sally, has made me a very happy man.

Some of the poems in this collection were first published as follows.
Camilla Caterpillar, *Tongue Twisters and Tonsil Twizzlers*, Macmillan 1997;
Cool Cat, *Dark as a Midnight Dream*, Ed Fiona Waters, Evans 1998;
The Green Unicorn, *Performance Poems*, Ed Brian Moses, Southgate 1996;
Midnight Meeting, *World Book Day Poetry Book 2001*, Ed Gaby Morgan, Macmillan 2001;
Polar Bears and Penguins, *While Shepherds Washed Their Socks*, Ed David Orme, Macmillan 1997;
Shark Attack, *A Sea Creature Ate My Teacher*, Ed Brian Moses, Macmillan 2000;
Some Day, My Prince, *Young Hippo Magic Poems*, Ed Jennifer Curry, Scholastic 1997;
Tina, *Time for a Rhyme, Peculiar Pets*, Ed Brian Moses, Macmillan 2001;
Unrattled, *A Noisy Noise Annoys*, Ed Jennifer Curry, Bodley Head/Red Fox 1996;
The Dung Beetle, *Revolting Poems to Make You Squirm*, Ed Susie Gibbs, OUP 2006.

In addition, the following poems first appeared in *A Poetry Teacher's Toolkit, Books 1, 2, 3 & 4* by Mike Jubb and Colette Drifte, published by David Fulton: **Bare Back Riding, My Cat is Dead, Badgers, Flesh Creeper, Cats, The Slow Toad and the Fast Car, The Cliché Monster, Adagio e Presto.**

Apologies for any mistakes or omissions.